TAKE THE LEAD

C Edition

POP HiTS

Series Editor: Chris Harvey

Editorial, production and recording: Artemis Music Limited • Design and production: Space DPS Limited • Published 2002

IMP

International
MUSIC
Publications

A Guide to Notation

Note and Rest Values

This chart shows the most commonly used note values and rests.

Name of note (UK)	Semibreve	Minim	Crotchet	Quaver	Semiquaver
Name of note (USA)	Whole note	Half note	Quarter note	Eighth note	Sixteenth note
Note symbol	o	♩	♩	♪	♪
Rest symbol	▬	▬	𝄽	𝄾	𝄿
Value per beats	4	2	1	1/2	1/4

Repeat Bars

When you come to a double dotted bar, you should repeat the music between the beginning of the piece and the repeat mark.

When you come to a repeat bar you should play again the music that is between the two dotted bars. 𝄆 𝄇

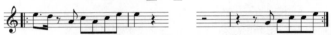

First, second and third endings

The first time through you should play the first ending until you see the repeat bar. Play the music again and skip the first time ending to play the second time ending, and so on.

D.C. (Da Capo)

When you come to this sign you should return to the beginning of the piece.

D.C. al Fine

When this sign appears, go back to the beginning and play through to the *Fine* ending marked. When playing a *D.C. al Fine*, you should ignore all repeat bars and first time endings.

D.S. (Dal Segno)

Go back to the 𝄋 sign.

D.S. al Fine

Go to the sign 𝄋 and play the ending labelled *(Fine)*.

D.S. al Coda

Repeat the music from the 𝄋 sign until the ⊕ or *To Coda* signs, and then go to the coda sign. Again, when playing through a *D. 𝄋 al Coda*, ignore all repeats and don't play the first time ending.

Accidentals

Flat ♭ - When a note has a flat sign before it, it should be played a semi tone lower.

Sharp ♯ - When a note has a sharp sign before it, it should be played a semi tone higher.

Natural ♮ - When a note has a natural sign before it, it usually indicates that a previous flat or sharp has been cancelled and that it should be played at it's actual pitch.

Bar Numbers

Bar numbers are used as a method of identification, usually as a point of reference in rehearsal. A bar may have more than one number if it is repeated within a piece.

Pause Sign

A pause is most commonly used to indicate that a note/chord should be extended in length at the player's discretion. It may also indicate a period of silence or the end of a piece.

Dynamic Markings

Dynamic markings show the volume at which certain notes or passages of music should be played. For example

pp	= very quiet	*mf*	= moderately loud
p	= quiet	*f*	= loud
mp	= moderately quiet	*ff*	= very loud

Time Signatures

Time signatures indicate the value of the notes and the number of beats in each bar.

The top number shows the number of beats in the bar and the bottom number shows the value of the note.

Introduction

Welcome to **TAKE THE LEAD *PLUS*: POP HITS**, part of an instrumental series that provides both young and not-so-young players with well-known songs and tunes as two-part arrangements. You will find that both parts have been arranged in a way that ensures playing either part is interesting and musically satisfying.

All eight pieces have been carefully selected and arranged at an easy level, and you will also find that the arrangements can be used with any number of instruments from the other editions in the series – B♭, E♭ and Bass Clef.

The professionally recorded backing CD provides an authentic accompaniment for both parts to play along with.

Wherever possible, we have simplified the more tricky rhythms. Also, we have kept marks of expression to a minimum, but feel free to experiment with these.

Above all, have fun and enjoy the experience of making music together.

Can't Fight The Moonlight

Words and Music by
Diane Warren

5

Backing

Can't Get You Out Of My Head

Words and Music by
Cathy Dennis and Robert Davis

Eternity

Words and Music by
Robert Williams and Guy Chambers

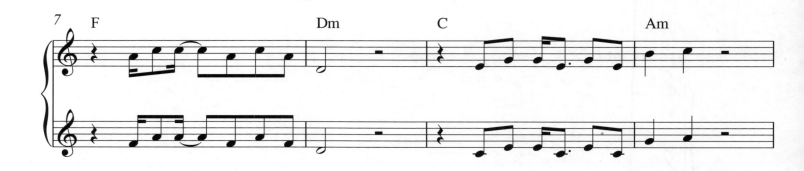

Handbags And Gladrags

Words and Music by
Mike D'Abo

Backing

I Want Love

Words by Bernie Taupin
Music by Elton John

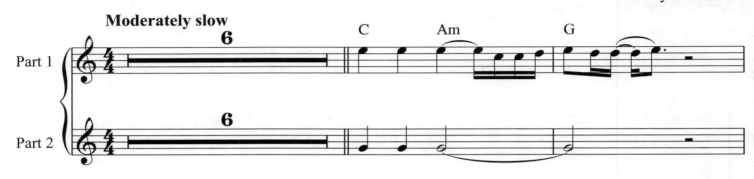

Backing

Fallin'

Words and Music by
Alicia Augello-Cook

Track 8
Backing

It's Raining Men

Words and Music by
Paul Jabara and Paul Shaffer

What If

Words and Music by
Steve Mac and Wayne Hector